Dedicated To Our Children

*Bert and Donna Pilgrim, and our
granddaughter, Alexandria*

Sheri Pace

Stacy and Christie Shirey

Contents

Preface

I have had the privilege of visiting the Holy Land four times. On those four trips I have discovered one of the most meaningful sites is in the old city of Jerusalem at the Convent of the Sisters of Zion. Down in the basement, which was excavated during the years 1931-37, was found the old courtyard of the Antonia. This was a military fortress named for Mark Anthony, which housed the Roman army. Carved into the stone pavement is the design of the King's Game, which Roman soldiers played while waiting for Jesus to come from his appearance before Pontius Pilate. There is also an ancient Roman gate nearby. Both of these places are called "Ecce Homo." The words mean "Behold the Man." Those are the words Pilate spoke of Jesus.

Every time I visit there I think about the meaning of those words, "Behold the man." On one of my visits the sermons in this series had their beginning.

I realized that this is one of the purposes of the season of Lent. It is a time for us to behold the Man, to think about him, to know him, to see him clearly. That is the purpose behind these messages.

There is something else also. It is never enough to just behold him. Those people who were there with him that fateful night beheld him. But that was all they did. Something else is needed. After we behold him, we then must make some decision about him.

I hope these messages will enable those who read them to behold the Man, and then to follow him more closely.

I want to thank the members of my congregation for their attention and response to this series. I want to thank my family and friends for their encouragement in the ministry of writing. Most of all, I want to thank my wife Shirley for her steadfast love, her constant support and her inspiration, which have enabled me to behold the Man.

Thomas A. Pilgrim
Memorial Day, 1995

"Behold The Man Who Was Tempted As We Are"

A man who owned a small town grocery store saw a little boy come in one afternoon. The little fellow stood near the front door looking at a barrel of apples. He would look up at the man and back down at the apples. Finally, the man went over and said to him, "Son, are you trying to steal one of those apples?" The boy replied, "No, sir. I'm trying to keep from it."

There are times in our lives when we are tempted to be less than we are. There are times when we are faced with the possibility of settling for less than the best; when we are more concerned with reaching goals than how we reach them; when we think that all that matters is results.

Today is the First Sunday of Lent. On these Sundays we will be thinking about Jesus heading toward Jerusalem. As we do this, I remind you of the words of Pilate as Jesus was brought out wearing a crown of thorns and a purple robe, "Behold the Man!" Today we look at Jesus at the very beginning of his ministry. Behold the man who was tempted as we are.

9

One day the carpenter laid down his tools and walked out of his shop. He went down that little dusty street out to the edge of town, and took that road which headed south. He went down along the Jordan River where his cousin John the Baptist was holding a meeting. There with the other folks he was baptized in Jordan creek. Then he went back up into the hills where, as Matthew tells us, "Behold, angels came and ministered to him."

The time had come for him to begin his ministry of proclaiming the Kingdom of God. But before he began this work, it was important for him to be alone for a while to decide exactly how he would carry out his mission. It was during that time that he faced what we call "the temptations of Jesus," when he had to choose what to do and how to do it, when he was faced with great decisions about his life's work.

Since Jesus was alone, there were no eyewitnesses, and what we have here in the gospels is the account Jesus gave his disciples about this experience. He told them what happened and how he felt.

He described that incident in vivid terms. He gave them a picturesque description of the inner tension, the pulling-apartness of great decisions as he tried to choose his method and his message. Can you imagine him at the end of that time standing on the Mount of Temptation looking back up toward Jerusalem?

I have been to that place several times. When I stand on the tell at old Jericho and look at that mountain I remember the words from a song in a Broadway play, "On a clear day you can see forever." I think about Jesus being there at the end of those 40 days looking out toward forever.

The temptations Jesus experienced at that time were real temptations. We sometimes think Jesus knew nothing of the things we face. But the writer of Hebrews reminds us that Jesus was "tempted in all points like as we are." His temptations are described in the gospels as being a struggle with the devil.

Jesus, of course, was never tempted to commit murder, mayhem, or immorality. The temptations he faced were more subtle than that. They had to do with the wrong use of his powers, giving in to easy solutions, achieving great ends by means which were below him and what he stood for.

Are not those the temptations most of us face these days? Few of us would be tempted to commit some real crime. We go by the bank every day without ever considering an illegal withdrawal at gunpoint. I have never thought of smuggling a gallon of milk out of the store under my coat.

Back in the days of the Old West an outlaw boarded a train. He said to the frightened passengers, "I'm going to rob every man and kiss every woman on this train." A gentleman stood up and said, "Sir, you can rob the men, but you're not going to kiss these ladies." One lady spoke up and said, "Now, you leave him alone. He's the one who's robbing this train."

Those are not the temptations we face. But we are faced with those subtle temptations to be less than we are. We are tempted to seek popularity, to be comfortable, to never go against the grain, to see only our side, to live for what we will eat and drink and wear, and to never look beyond any of that. We are tempted to reduce life to its lowest level — survival. In doing that we become less than we are.

How do we face such temptations? The answer lies in the way Jesus faced his own temptations, for he was tempted as we are.

*   *   *

First, he understood the deepest hungers of the human heart. Jesus had been fasting in the wilderness 40 days. When he came to the end of that period of thought and reflection he was hungry. He heard those devilish words, "If you are the Son of God, command this stone to become bread."

Jesus was tempted to use his powers to satisfy his own hunger. But there was more to it. It was not just the matter of his own hunger. Even as we are moved with compassion for those who are without food today, so Jesus was concerned for the hungry people of his own time. How easy it would have

11

been for him to respond to that by providing food for them all! There were many people who would have been willing to follow any person who could supply bread. He could have easily won a following this way. But this was not the way for him to choose. He knew he must not use bread in this way.

How easy it would have been for Jesus to yield to that temptation! He was the Son of God being tempted to become a magician. That was far below him. He knew the real hungers were much deeper than that. He knew the real need was for bread which came from Heaven. And so, he answered, "Man shall not live by bread alone, but by every word of God."

You see, here is one of the problems we continually face. Whenever we forget the deepest hungers of the human heart, we become less than we are.

Oh, we have amassed a great assortment of things which do not satisfy. Over the last few decades we have been led to believe that we must have more and more. But the more we have, the greater our hunger becomes for the things which do not satisfy the deepest hungers of the human heart. And so, we become less than we are because we live for things which are below us. But those are not the things we really want.

A young man graduated from college. His father threw a great party for him out at their farm and invited everyone to come. As part of the entertainment he filled the swimming pool with alligators and said to all the young men, "Anyone who swims across this pool can have this farm, or all my money, or the hand of my daughter in marriage." Just then a young man hit the water, and swam across the pool, and jumped out on the other side. The man ran around to him and asked, "What do you want, this farm, my money, or the hand of my daughter?" He said, "I want the guy who pushed me in this pool."

What is it we really want? Isn't it something far richer than what we can possess?

A work crew in India was repairing a railroad near a small town. On a train coming toward them was a Hindu who had found a New Testament. He read some of it and then tore it up and threw the scraps of paper out the window just as the train went by the work crew. One of the workers saw the little pieces of paper floating to the ground. He picked one of them up and saw the words, "Bread of Life." He knew that was what he needed, Bread of Life. He went into town and found the Christian church. There he was served the Bread which satisfies.[1]

Jesus said, "I am the bread of life. He who comes to me shall never hunger, and he who believes in me shall never thirst."

He fulfills the deepest hungers of the human heart.

* * *

Second, Jesus knew the importance of keeping God in his rightful place. Here is the second temptation. The devil offered Jesus all the kingdoms of the world if he would worship him. He said, "If you will worship before me, all will be yours."

In Palestine in those days there was a great deal of unrest, as there is today. There were many people who wanted to overthrow the Romans, start a war, and drive them into the sea. They were waiting for the Messiah to come and lead them in this kind of campaign. If Jesus had only spoken the word, he could have become that kind of leader. He could have become the political savior of Israel, the new King of the Jews. But, no, Jesus knew the kingdom he represented, the Kingdom of God, was much greater and more far-reaching than any political kingdom. He refused to take up the sword and become a political savior.

So he answered the devil, "You shall worship the Lord your God, and Him only you shall serve."

We become less than we are when we forget that. This is one of our major problems today, filled with such dangerous possibilities.

At the outbreak of World War II Winston Churchill said, "Someone took Mussolini to the top of the mountain, and showed him all the kingdoms of the world."

That continues to be a problem in our world today. But this does not happen to our enemies only. It happens to us as well. Our lives become filled with dangerous possibilities whenever we fail to keep God in his rightful place.

When any of us loses sight of that fact we become less than we are. But when we do keep God in his rightful place in our lives, our hearts, our plans, then life is in God's hands, and we need not worry about what God will do with us.

Back in the 1950s Alan Walker, a Methodist preacher in Australia, gave up his church to lead a preaching mission there. He also came to the United States to preach in a number of places. As he prepared to return home, he had no church and the future seemed to be uncertain. He was invited to become the pastor of several large American churches. But he did not feel it was the thing to do. On the way home he received word he would be sent to a church in Sydney. He would do his greatest work there. He said he felt God was a part of those decisions, and that God gave him the work to do in Sydney.[2]

Jesus had that same conviction. He knew that God would open up the way and lead him where he should be going. We can know that if we keep God in his rightful place.

* * *

Finally, in facing temptation, Jesus realized there were no shortcuts to where he must go. There was no easy way for him to reach his destiny. And yet, there was still that nagging voice, "If you are the Son of God, throw yourself down from here."

Jesus knew, however, there could be no shortcuts, no easy way out, no favoritism because he was the Son of God. So he replied, "You shall not tempt the Lord your God."

Instead he would travel the long, lonely, difficult road to the cross. He would not become less than God's Son by trying to avoid all that life was to mean to him. He had a mission to carry out, the necessary and inescapable result of which would be an agonizing death on a cross in shame and dishonor. There was no way around that, no way to avoid that.

14

There are no shortcuts for us either. There is no easy way out of life's dangerous and difficult situations. If Jesus had to bear a cross, we need not expect anything else. This will call for courage on our part.

A young lady whose father was a general in the army was to marry an officer. She begged her father to promote him, knowing he would not want her married to such a low-ranking officer. He said, "I can't promote him. But if he's going to marry you, he does deserve a medal for bravery."

We need courage. But even more than that we need the kind of courage which comes out of faith in God, for there are times when this courage we muster up gives way, runs out, is not enough. We need the kind of courage which is the result of faith in God, for there are no easy ways for us to be disciples of Jesus Christ today, no shortcuts to where he would lead us.

When the Salvation Army first went to India, the British authorities were concerned and issued orders that they were to hold no open meetings or marches through the streets. But Commissioner Tucker knew they must not obey such an order. So one day they came marching down the street. They were met by soldiers. An officer said, "In the name of her Majesty, Queen of England, I order you to disperse." And Tucker answered, "In the name of His majesty, the King of Kings and Lord of Lords, I command you to stand aside." They stood aside.[3]

One day Jesus said to those temptations he faced, "Stand aside." Because he did, you and I can say to everything which tempts us and to every form of hatred, bigotry, and ignorance, "In the name of the King of kings stand aside." And they will stand aside.

---

1. Leslie D. Weatherhead, *Over His Own Signature,* Abingdon Press, New York, Nashville, 1955, p. 25.

15

2. Alan Walker, *Jesus The Liberator,* Abingdon Press, Nashville, New York, 1973, p. 124.

3. Walker, *Ibid.,* p. 78.

Almighty God, who is the hope of all who believe and the help of all who trust, we gather here to worship thee, for thou art the hope of the world and the help of all humankind.

On this First Sunday in the season of Lent enable us to begin a journey that will lead us to behold the Man. Lead us to the knowledge that as Jesus faced temptation he identified himself with us, and was tempted in all points like as we are.

O God, we offer to thee our worship, our prayers of thanksgiving and our songs of praise, for all thou hast done for us. For thy bountiful blessings upon us, for all thy gifts of love, mercy and grace we thank thee, O God.

We give thee our gratitude, our worship, our service, not out of any sense of obligation, but because of our love for thee, for thy ways, for thy kingdom and because thou hast laid thy hands upon us and called us by name, given us a new name and made us thy children.

Continue to be at work in our lives, and give us all the faith we need. Make us to be people of courage and hope, even in the face of some of the things which some of us are up against.

Be with those of our church family and community who bear special burdens, who are sick, or who may be in sorrow. Bless them, and help them, and may they know of thy love and our love.

We make this our prayer in the name of thy Son and our Savior. Amen.

"An Apple A Day"
Object: an apple

Good morning, boys and girls. I am so glad you have come to Sunday school and church today. This is a special day. Who knows what it is? It is the First Sunday in Lent. This is a time leading up to Easter Sunday. On these Sundays we are thinking about Jesus on his way to the cross in Jerusalem. Today we are thinking about the temptations of Jesus.

Look at this. Who knows a saying we use about apples? That is right. An apple a day keeps the doctor away.

There is a story at the beginning of the Bible about Adam and Eve being tempted by the devil to eat some fruit from a tree God told them not to touch. The devil tempted them. He said, "Go ahead; it will not hurt you. You will like it." So, they ate and had to leave the garden. I think you know this story well.

Jesus had a time when the devil tempted him also. He was tempted to use his powers for his own welfare. But he did not give in to that. He said, "Get behind me, Satan. Worship only God." Jesus remained strong and did not give in.

I think for most of us there is an apple a day. There is a temptation every day, often more than one a day, to do something God would not want us to do. A temptation a day we give in to keeps *us* away. It keeps us away from God and those we love.

But, we can be like Jesus as we face temptation. We can keep our faces turned toward God and be true to God. We can live the way God wants us to live, and be his children.

May we pray. O God, help us to keep our eyes upon you, and always be strong for you, in Jesus' name. Amen.

Prelude

Chiming Of The Hour

Introit

The Hymn Of Praise "O Worship The King"

Affirmation Of Faith The Apostles' Creed

Invocation

Moments Of Fellowship

Pastoral Prayer And The Lord's Prayer

The Children's Message "An Apple A Day"

The Anthem "I Will Remember Thee"

The Prayer Of Dedication

The Offertory

The Doxology

The Hymn Of Preparation "O For A Faith That Will Not Shrink"

Scripture Lesson Luke 4:1-13

Sermon "Behold The Man Who Was Tempted As We Are"

Invitation To Christian Discipleship

Hymn Of Invitation "Be Thou My Vision"

Benediction

The Choral Response

Postlude

1. Have someone read the scripture lesson again: Luke 4:1-13.

2. What did Jesus do in the face of temptation?

3. What are the temptations you face?

4. How do you respond to the things which tempt you?

5. What is the real danger of temptation?

6. Share the value of prayer in the face of temptation.

7. When are our temptations really faced and overcome?

Close with each person saying a sentence prayer asking for the strength to overcome temptation.

"Behold The Man Who Takes Away Sin"

G. K. Chesterton was once asked the question, "Why did you join the church so late in life?" He answered, "To get rid of my sins."[1]

That is a wonderful answer. It is still the solution for so many of the world's problems and the problems of people everywhere. So many of us know that there is something wrong, something which must be set right at some point along the way. And we want someone to set things right. Yet, many times we have the feeling that we cannot break through, cannot make the connection, cannot find the right formula.

Harold Kushner, in his book *Who Needs God*, tells about a television drama in which a man dies and finds himself standing in line. There is an usher there telling people which way to go, through one door or another. One door leads to heaven and the other door leads to hell. The man says to the usher, "You mean I can choose either one? There is no judgment, no taking account of how I lived?" The usher tells him that is right and to move along. The man says, "But, I want to confess; I want to come clean; I want to be judged." The

21

usher responds, "We don't have time for that. Just choose a door and move along." The man decides to go through the door to hell. He wanted to be judged.[2]

Yes, we know we need someone or something out beyond us to set things straight. At this point, enter Jesus of Nazareth. Behold the man who takes away sin.

Some people thought it was the Baptist who came to do that. But John quickly let it be known that he was not the Christ. It would be another who would come after him. And so, one day when John was preaching there in the wilderness along the Jordan River, he saw Jesus coming toward him. John knew he was the one. So he pointed to Jesus and said to the people, "Behold! The Lamb of God who takes away the sin of the world!"

In this season of Lent as we think about Jesus heading toward Jerusalem and the cross, we know he came to do many things. One of those things he came to do was to restore a right relationship between God and his children. John the Baptist knew it right off, "Behold the Lamb of God who takes away the sin of the world."

We see it in many places later in the story. Jesus was announcing and granting God's forgiveness long before he even got to the cross.

In Capernaum a crippled man was let down through the ceiling to where Jesus was preaching. Jesus said to the man, "Your sins are forgiven . . . Take up your bed and go home." A woman was about to be stoned to death for adultery. Jesus stopped the crowd and said to her, "Neither do I condemn you. Go and sin no more." Late in the night Nicodemus came to see Jesus. Jesus said to him, "You must be born anew."

In all of those incidents and in so many more, we see Jesus calling people away from their sins. But it is not just a matter of them working it out for themselves. The whole point of the New Testament is that Jesus came to do for us what none of us can do for ourselves. He came to take away the sins of the world. Look at some things involved in this.

*   *   *

Jesus came to reveal a forgiving God. That is the nature of God. God forgives.

John told the people that day he had not known who Jesus was, but he knew "He should be revealed to Israel." This is the one, John was saying.

It is so basic in the New Testament: "God so loved the world that He gave His only begotten Son that whoever believes in Him should not perish, but have everlasting life."

That is something so very basic in our understanding of what God is like. It is why John referred to Jesus as being the Lamb of God. The lamb was always sacrificed for the sins of the people. John said Jesus was "the Lamb of God who takes away the sin of the world."

Jesus came to reveal a forgiving God. He came to help us know how God is: that God loves his children and is even willing to give up his own Son for them to help them understand.

Everything Jesus said and did points to this truth. We see it in his words, his attitudes, his deeds, and his actions. We see it being demonstrated ultimately in the cross as he gives up his own life for the sin of the world. It is in this that we learn that God forgives, not because of any sacrifice we make, but because of the sacrifice Jesus himself was.

We all need this, for we know none of us can handle the way we are by ourselves.

When we were serving the church in Jefferson, Georgia, the phone rang in the office one morning. The voice on the other end said, "Is this Judge Smith's office?" I said, "No, this is the United Methodist Church." He replied, "Oh, I'm sorry." I answered, "It's all right. Maybe you need grace instead of law anyway." He laughed as he hung up the phone.

That is our need, the gracious forgiveness of God. We need this because we seek our own way and will instead of God's. We tend to put ourselves in God's place, thinking the world revolves around us and our own little wants and wishes. In our attempts to find a heaven, we wind up creating a hell. And we know we need a forgiving God.

One afternoon when I was a child, my brothers and I were having a dirt-clod war with some of the other kids in the neighborhood. There we were encamped in a ditch along the street which ran down beside our house. The enemy was up near the house in the bushes and behind those long back steps. At a crucial point one of my brothers stood up and fired a volley at them. The largest dirt-clod of all sailed through the sky. It was a thing of beauty to see as it went over the enemy, over the bushes and through the window of our bedroom. A truce was called and we ran inside. There was only one thing to do — pull down the shade and hope no one ever found out. But not long after that, it began to turn cold and we had to confess what we had done. Much to my surprise our parents forgave us immediately, with only some words like, "Take better aim next time." I never forgot that. I was always amazed at their capacity to forgive.

That is the way God is. And Jesus came to reveal a forgiving God.

*　*　*

Look further then at this. Jesus came to create a transforming friendship. You see, something happens when God forgives.

The next day after John pointed to Jesus, John was with two of his disciples. Again he saw Jesus and again he said, "Behold the Lamb of God." When the two disciples heard this, "they followed Jesus." Jesus turned around and said to them, "What do you seek?" They answered, "Rabbi, where are you staying?" That was the beginning of that band of disciples Jesus formed. They wanted to be with him, and he wanted them to follow him. Later on toward the end Jesus would say to all of them, "No longer do I call you servants. Now I call you my friends."

That friendship they shared reshaped the lives of the disciples. They had been rough men, weathered fishermen, shrewd businessmen, common men, sinners all. But the friendship of Jesus transformed them. Finally, when he went to the cross, they understood the words, "Greater love has no man than he who lays down his life for his friends."

The forgiveness of God they saw in the cross and in the friendship they had with Jesus transformed them, made them no longer just sinners, but sinners who became saints. There was a power in the friendship they shared with Jesus. That power made them want to be like him. He took the sin away from them and replaced it with forgiveness, love, compassion, mercy, and commitment, so much so that one day those who followed him even bore his name and were called "Christians." Jesus had told them, "Be imitators of me." They became like him.

That is a transforming friendship we still need today. The way of Jesus is simply the best way to live and get along in this world.

One time on *The Andy Griffith Show* Opie had been in a fight. Andy was trying to talk with him about it and how to get along with people. Andy said, "Sometimes you have to give something and expect nothing." Opie replied, "I did. I gave him a sock in the head." Andy said, "Well, you have to do things out of charity." Opie replied, "I didn't charge him nothing for it." Andy said, "You have to give just for the joy of it." Opie replied, "I enjoyed it."

Life will work only one way, and that is the way of Jesus. That is why the church is still important today. It holds before us the way of Jesus, and involves us in a transforming fellowship with him.

Albert Ritschel, one of the outstanding European theologians of many years ago, called the church "the fellowship of the forgiven."[3]

Benjamin West, the painter, said that when he was a small child his mother left him with his sister Sally while she went to the store. While she was gone he found some paint and decided to paint a picture of Sally. He made a terrible mess with the paint. But when his mother came in she did not say anything about the mess. She looked at the painting of his sister and said, "Why, it's Sally." And then she kissed him. He said, "My mother's kiss made me a painter."[4]

25

Just so, Jesus loved his disciples into being something they had never even imagined. He does the same for us through his transforming friendship.

* * *

Look finally at this. Jesus came to offer an exciting adventure. This is true because when God forgives and we enter a transforming friendship all of life takes a new direction.

Jesus gave those two disciples an invitation. They wanted to know where Jesus was going. They asked, "Where are you staying?" Jesus answered, "Come and see." And they went with him.

That makes life an exciting adventure. Jesus is always staying at the "come and see" place. He always calls us to "come and see," to join him at the "come and see" place, the place which is unknown but always filled with adventure.

He redirects our thinking. He gives us a new perspective on everything.

He takes a band of sinners and makes them his church. He sends them out with the gospel message to believe it, live it, share it, tell it, and demonstrate it.

He leads them to places they have never been which are yet unknown. He calls forth from them more than they ever knew was within them.

He takes away sin by being the sinner's friend. Then by dying for them, he makes them into messengers of the glad Good News. He sends them on an exciting adventure.

They bring all the world under the influence of Christ, his gospel, his kingdom, and they allow it to seep into the far corners of man's existence so that nothing can escape it.

Still Jesus calls us to this. Still he is there to uphold us, to guide us, and to lead us as we serve him and God's Kingdom.

On a Sunday in the summer of 1945, a German bishop was preparing to preach. But the Nazi soldiers came and arrested him and put him in prison. He knew he might not come out of that prison alive. When they put him in a cell he heard someone in another cell whistling the hymn, "O For A Thousand Tongues To Sing." He whistled back a line and they began to whistle that hymn together. He began to realize that he was not alone there in that cell. He knew the presence of Christ was with them to uphold them. With that knowledge he would endure.[5]

In that faith we will know we are in the hands of a forgiving God, held up by a transforming friendship, led forward on an exciting adventure.

---

1. George Thompson, "Kissing The Joy," *Pulpit Digest,* Harper, San Francisco, May-June, 1992, p. 22.

2. Harold Kushner, *Who Needs God,* Summit Books, New York, 1989, p. 75.

3. George Wesley Buchanon, "Wandering Toward Home," *Pulpit Digest,* Harper, San Francisco, March-April, 1993, p. 72.

4. Dennis R. Fakes, *Emphasis,* CSS Publishing Co., Lima, Ohio, March-April, 1993, p. 46.

5. William H. Hinson, *The Power Of Holy Habits,* Abingdon Press, Nashville, 1991, p. 45.

Eternal God and Father of all humankind, the source of all that is, our sustainer and friend, accept our thanksgiving for the ways our lives are blessed of thee.

In this season, O God, help us to draw closer to thy Son and our Savior, Jesus Christ, and to behold his goodness and greatness.

Father, we offer to thee our songs of praise because of all thy blessings upon us. We know thou hast showered us with all those things which make life worth living.

And, we offer to thee the best that is within us, through our service in this church. So, take from us, O God, these gifts we offer back to thee and use us for the work of thy Kingdom.

Take away our sins, and grant us thy forgiveness. Take away our doubts and our confusion, and give us the gift of faith. Take away the pain of our sorrows and suffering, and heal our brokenness.

Bless those of our church family and community who are in sorrow.

Bless thy world, O God. Help us to walk in the ways of peace, and give wisdom to the leaders of the world. Protect those who have no one to defend them. We ask all of this in the name of thy well-beloved Son. Amen.

"Having A Clean Slate"
Object: a small chalkboard

Good morning, boys and girls. It is good to see all of you here today. Now, today is the Second Sunday in Lent. Remember, this is a time leading up to Easter Sunday. We are thinking about Jesus going toward Jerusalem. Today we are thinking about forgiveness.

Now, let me show you this chalkboard. A long time ago children like you in school did not have paper tablets to write on, or computers. They had a small chalkboard, or a slate board. You can write on a chalkboard a word like this, "c e t." Oh, no! I made a mistake. Let's erase this and start over. "C a t" is what I meant to write. This is where we got the saying, "a clean slate." It means today to be able to begin again, to start over, to correct a mistake.

In our scripture lesson today we will read about John the Baptist pointing to Jesus and saying, "Behold the Lamb of God, who takes away the sins of the world." That means Jesus is the one who helps us correct our mistakes. He wipes the slate clean. He erases the wrong things we do. He forgives us when we do things we should not do. He brings to us the forgiveness of God.

All of us make mistakes and do wrong things. But God loves us. That is why he sent us Jesus, his Son: to tell us about God's love and forgiveness. And to wipe the slate clean, to erase the wrong things we do.

May we pray. O God, thank you for your Son who brings to us your forgiveness. Amen.

Prelude

Chiming Of The Hour

Introit

The Hymn Of Praise "Amazing Grace"

Affirmation Of Faith   The Apostles' Creed

Invocation

Moments Of Fellowship

Pastoral Prayer And The Lord's Prayer

The Children's Message "Having A Clean Slate"

The Anthem "Glorify God"

The Prayer Of Dedication

The Offertory

The Doxology

The Hymn Of Preparation "Alas! And Did My Savior Bleed"

Scripture Lesson John 1:29-39

Sermon "Behold The Man Who Takes Away Sin"

Invitation To Christian Discipleship

Hymn Of Invitation "Beneath The Cross Of Jesus"

Benediction

The Choral Response

Postlude

1. Have someone read the scripture lesson again: John 1:29-39. Spend a few minutes sharing the significance of this event at the time it took place.

2. Let each person share briefly what these words mean to him or her.

3. Why do we need God's forgiveness?

4. What is necessary in order to receive God's forgiveness?

5. How do we respond to this forgiveness?

6. How does this forgiveness of God affect our relationships with other people?

7. Share ways of showing forgiveness.

Close with a time of praying by several people, and then pray together the Lord's Prayer.

"Behold The Man Who Taught By The Sea"

It was the end of the school year and a first grade teacher was saying good-bye to her students. One little boy said to her, "Teacher, I sure do like you. I'd like to stay in the first grade forever, but I've been promoted. Boy, I wish you knew enough to teach me in the second grade."[1]

So many people who are successful are able to look back at a person who first turned on a light inside the mind, who quickened the thinking, who first stirred the desire to learn. Behind every successful person there is the teacher. Most of us can look back across the years and remember such a person.

I can remember Sunday school teachers in my childhood years. I remember the songs we sang, the lady who played the piano and was so happy about it, the cookies they gave us, the warm feeling they created which caused me to think of Sunday school as a wonderful place to be.

I remember a teacher in college who first introduced me to Paul Tillich and Karl Barth, and opened up a world of new insight and understanding.

I remember a teacher in seminary who convinced me I could learn how to be the best possible preacher.

I remember the many teachers I met through their books as I sat on the porch of a country parsonage, which was my only office, on warm summer mornings and had my mind inspired.

Most of us can remember a person who helped us understand what it means to be taught. But, we also know that not every one has the gift of teaching.

Yogi Berra was a great ballplayer with the Yankees. He was the Most Valuable Player in the American League three times. But he was not as successful as a manager. One of his players once said, "Yogi knows more about baseball than all of the team put together. It's too bad he doesn't know how to tell us about it."[2] Yogi has become famous for unclear noncommunication. He is not a teacher.

Elton Trueblood was a well-known Christian teacher, preacher, and writer. After he retired he published a book of essays under the title, *The Teacher*. The title, he said, described his vocation for half a century.[3]

Jesus was the master teacher. In a world which can so easily lose its way and in a time of such moral confusion — behold the Man who taught by the sea.

William Barclay points out that in the New Testament gospels we find several titles for Jesus. He is called Rabbi, Teacher, and Master more than 50 times. All three titles really mean "Teacher."[4]

Jesus was the greatest teacher. No one ever spoke the way he did. He understood clearly the motives, the hopes, the dreams, the fears and the frustrations of those to whom he spoke.

Most of his teaching ministry took place up in Galilee, centered around the city of Capernaum where he made his headquarters. We know that in all those towns he visited he taught in the synagogues. But there were some places where the crowds were so great that he could only address them in the open air. One such occasion is reported to us in what we call the Sermon on the Mount.

Here in our lesson for today in Mark, chapter 4, we find Jesus teaching by the sea. So many people came to hear him that he had to get in a boat and speak to them from the water's edge. In this passage we find some key elements about the teaching of Jesus.

Now, the whole season of Lent, moving toward Easter, reminds us that were it not for the death and resurrection of Jesus we would know nothing of his teaching. Yet because of his death and resurrection his teaching has authority and is the only way to live. He is the ultimate teacher and his words are the words of life. Let us examine some key elements about his teaching.

* * *

His teaching attracted the crowds. That is the first thing which strikes us about the teaching of Jesus. Mark tells us here in this passage that "a great multitude was gathered to him, so that he got into a boat and sat in it on the sea; and the whole multitude was on the land facing the sea." So many people came to hear him, thousands of them, that he was being pushed by them on the edge of the lake. To keep from being pushed in the water, he got in the boat and sat there speaking to that great multitude of people.

Why did that happen? What caused those people to come there? Why was it that everywhere he went people wanted to hear him?

It was not that this was something new, the latest form of entertainment, a way to pass the time, or some new diversion. There were many traveling preachers, magicians and exorcists who traveled up and down the highways and byways. Jesus was not just another in a long line of wise counselors. No, there was something else different about him.

One thing was that magnetic personality which drew other people to him. He looked at people the way no one ever had. He communicated his concern for them. They wanted to be close to him.

Another thing was the fact that there was something so appealing in what he said. He spoke words of hope, comfort, rebuke, and encouragement, words of life. They are still words of life for us today. We still need to hear the things he said. He still speaks clearly to us.

A farmer went into town one night to hear a political candidate for a state office. When the farmer returned home his wife asked him what the man had talked about. The farmer scratched his head and replied, "He didn't say."

It was never that way with Jesus. The message of Jesus is clear. Those words still speak to us. We are drawn to them. We know that as he speaks of God, faith, courage, joy and life he is speaking to us where we live. And we know we need his words in order to live.

As Simon Peter confessed, "Lord, to whom shall we go? Only you have the words of life."

In 1942 W. A. Smart, a theology professor at Emory University, published *The Contemporary Christ*. At the end of that book he wrote about how we think of Christ as belonging to first century Palestine. But then we discover him walking with us and we hear what he says. We hear him speak the homely things of his long-ago world and we know these are "the things by which our world must live if it would escape the abyss."⁵ His words still draw us to him.

* * *

His teaching contained a call. That is a second striking thing about the teaching of Jesus. Mark states, "Then he taught them many things by parables." The first parable Mark relates is what we call the parable of the soil. It is a simple story about a farmer sowing seed. Jesus pictures him walking through a field, and as he sows the seed some of it falls by the way and the birds eat it. Some of it falls among the rocks and cannot take hold. Some of it falls among the thorns which choke the sprouts. But some seeds fall into good soil and they produce a fine crop.

A man from the city decided he wanted to change his way of living and become a chicken farmer. So he bought an old run-down farm, moved out there, cleaned it up, bought 100 baby chicks and planted them head down. But nothing happened. Then, he bought 100 more and planted them head up, feet down. Nothing happened. He called the county agent, who came out to see him. He explained the problem to the county agent. After thinking a minute the county agent asked, "Have you had your soil tested?"

Jesus was saying in this parable that people who hear what he says will be like these kinds of soil. His words will take root in the lives of some and it will bear fruit in the Kingdom of God.

Most of the teaching of Jesus was in the form of these parables.

George Buttrick, the great Presbyterian preacher, wrote a book about the parables of Jesus. He pointed out that these parables were plain stories spoken to common people. They were stories about life. They did not have some great hidden meaning.[6]

C. H. Dodd, a New Testament scholar, said of these parables, "They are the natural expression of a mind that sees truth in concrete pictures rather than conceives it in abstractions."[7]

So Jesus was a storyteller. He chose to speak to people with these little stories about the common, everyday things they understood. In fact at one point the gospels say, "From then on he spoke to them only in parables."

These parables had a purpose. They were meant to call people into the Kingdom of God. In so many places we hear Jesus saying, "The Kingdom of God is like . . . ." Then he draws a picture with words.

Now not all of the things Jesus said were original. He borrowed some things he said. However, many of his parables were original stories he took from life.

These stories Jesus told are the greatest stories ever told. Who could ever forget the parables of the Prodigal Son, the Good Samaritan, the Mustard Seed, the Pearl of Great Price? No such stories were ever told by anyone before or since.

These stories contained a call to citizenship in the Kingdom of God. Jesus called people to live in God's Kingdom, and to allow the Kingdom of God to live in them. He called them to look around and see it everywhere, and to anticipate its coming. He called them to realize the Kingdom's great power, and to submit their lives to the rule of God.

This is a call we must continue to heed. We are still called to come live in the Kingdom of God, and to allow the Kingdom of God to live in us.

In a children's Sunday school class all the children were singing, "Praise him, Praise him, All ye little children." They sang through that song, which also contains the verses, "Love him, Love him" and "Serve him, Serve him!" At that point they heard someone announce that refreshments were being served in the kitchen. They started to leave their room, but one little boy said, "We forgot to crown him!" They all came back in the room and finished the song, "Crown him, Crown him, All ye little children."[8] We are still called today to crown him King and become citizens of his Kingdom.

*　*　*

His teaching offered a challenge. That is the third striking thing about his teaching. Mark tells us that at this point, "He said to them, 'He who has ears to hear, let him hear!'" Jesus was saying, "Listen! Have ears that will listen. And then, do something about this. Let what I say take root in your life."

He was telling those people who came to hear him that they would have to decide which kind of soil they would be like. They would have to let his words live in them.

A lady was talking with her doctor. He asked how things were going, and if she had any problems. She said, "Nothing medical. But, you know I live alone and sometimes I hear people running through my house at night." He said, "Let me see. You are hearing your own heartbeat. You have your hearing aid in backward."

A man went in a restaurant and saw a sign which said, "We will serve anything you order." He thought about that and decided to see. He said to the waiter, "I'll have an elephant ear sandwich." The waiter replied, "Coming right up." In a minute the waiter came back and told him he could not serve him that. The man said, "That's what I thought!" The waiter answered, "Oh, we have the elephant ears. We're just out of that big ole bread!"

Here is the challenge for us today — using the ears we have and catching the ear of our society. The Christian gospel has a difficult time getting through the clamor of today. Most people are being bombarded by words and information. The age of communication makes communicating some things quite difficult. But, those who have ears to hear — listen!

Would you listen to what Jesus has to say to us today? Would you receive what he says in the sense that you will let it filter through and speak to your heart and mind, your way of thinking, your way of living, your values and ideals, your way of making decisions, who you are and what you have? Would you become good soil that is fertile so a tiny seed of what he says can take root in your life, spring up and bear much fruit in the Kingdom of God?

A college student named Fred Smith wrote a paper on developing an overnight parcel delivery system. His professor did not like the idea and gave him a "C" on the paper. But that idea kept growing in Fred Smith's mind. He transformed the idea into a $4 billion business which he called "Federal Express."

Some wonderful things happen when we get in our thinking the teaching of Jesus and the things he said about the Kingdom of God. Somebody else begins to see that Kingdom living in us.

Bishop Ernest Fitzgerald told the story about the woman who saw a little boy who had no shoes. It was a cold winter day, and her heart went out to him. She bought him some shoes to wear. At first the boy went running off without saying thank you. She was disappointed about that, but suddenly he was back. He said, "Lady, I forgot to thank you for my shoes, and I want to ask you a question. Are you God's wife?" She was surprised by that, but managed to say, "No, I'm just one of his children." To that the boy replied, "Well, I knew you were kin to him in some way."[9]

Marvelous things happen when we hear what Jesus is saying. I know all of you have ears. Are you listening?

---

1. Lloyd J. Ogilvie, *Ask Him Anything,* Word, Inc., Waco, Texas, 1981, p. 94.

2. Bruce Larson, *Setting Men Free,* Zondervan Publishing House, Grand Rapids, Michigan, 1967, p. 53.

3. D. Elton Trueblood, *The Teacher,* Broadman Press, Nashville, Tennessee, 1980, p. 9.

4. William Barclay, *The Mind of Jesus,* Harper & Row Publishers, New York and Evanston, 1960, p. 89.

5. W. A. Smart, *The Contemporary Christ,* Abingdon-Cokesbury Press, New York-Nashville, 1942, p. 163.

6. George Buttrick, *The Parables of Jesus,* Harper & Row Publishers, New York and London, 1928, p. xxv.

7. C. H. Dodd, *The Parables of the Kingdom,* Charles Scribner's Sons, New York, 1961, p. 5.

8. John Thomas Randolph, "What You Need Is What You See," *Emphasis,* CSS Publishing, Lima, Ohio, January-February, 1993, p. 67.

9. Ernest A. Fitzgerald, *Diamonds Everywhere,* Abingdon Press, Nashville, 1983, p. 52.

Our Father, we gather today to worship and serve thee and to give ourselves to thee. Accept our thanksgiving and speak to us in this time together.

We thank thee, gracious God, for all thy rich blessings upon us. For thy goodness we see at work in our lives, we thank thee. For thy hand of mercy and graciousness and bounty, we thank thee, O God.

We thank thee for the gift of thy Son and our Savior, Jesus Christ. During this season of Lent we follow him along those roads which led him toward Jerusalem and the cross. Prepare our hearts and minds to suffer with him that we may know the true joy of resurrection.

We thank thee, O God, for this church and for the call to serve thy Kingdom here. We are thankful for all who give themselves in the mission and ministry of this church. Bless us as we teach and learn here the ways of thy Kingdom.

Forgive our sins, merciful God. Give all of us faith and hope and love. Help us to be renewed in our faith in these days. May we continue to hear the voice of Christ calling us onward, outward, and upward.

Heal our sick, and keep thy hands upon them. Be with those who are alone and afraid. Comfort all who mourn.

Be with suffering people the world over. Use us in the answering of prayers for hurting people everywhere.

We make this prayer in the name of thy Son, Jesus Christ. Amen.

"Everybody Loves A Story"
Object: a children's book

Good morning, boys and girls. Welcome to our story time. I am so glad to see each of you here today. Now, today is the Third Sunday in Lent. As we think about Jesus on the way to Jerusalem I want us today to look at Jesus and the way he taught people. Jesus was a teacher. People called him a "Rabbi." He called his closest followers "Disciples." That word means "students." So, they were trying to learn his way. He taught about God, God's Kingdom or rule in our lives, faith, love, and service to God. He had a special way of teaching.

Look at this book. Everybody read the title together, *The Cat In The Hat.* That's right. This is a book most all of us love. All of us love stories, don't we? Everybody loves a story. Young people and old people, little people and big people, all people love a good story. That is why we read books and watch television and go to movies.

Jesus told a special kind of story called a "parable." This was a story with a special meaning about God and God's kingdom. I want you to listen closely to the scripture lesson today. There is a story in it Jesus told. The point of that story is that we must let the Good News we hear in the things Jesus said take root in our lives and live and grow. So, don't just listen and love the story. Let the truth of Jesus' words live in you.

May we pray. O God, help us to hear the stories of Jesus and open our hearts to him. Amen.

Prelude

Chiming Of The Hour

Introit

The Hymn Of Praise "To God Be The Glory"

Affirmation Of Faith   The Apostles' Creed

Invocation

Moments Of Fellowship

Pastoral Prayer And The Lord's Prayer

The Children's Message "Everybody Loves A Story"

The Anthem "The Earth Is The Lord's"

The Prayer Of Dedication

The Offertory

The Doxology

The Hymn Of Preparation "Near To The Heart Of God"

Scripture Lesson Mark 4:1-9

Sermon "Behold The Man Who Taught By The Sea"

Invitation To Christian Discipleship

Hymn Of Invitation "Jesus Is All The World To Me"

Benediction

The Choral Response

Postlude

1. Have someone read the scripture lesson again: Mark 4:1-9.

2. Share with the group the significance of a teacher who influenced you. What difference did this make in your life?

3. What is different about the teaching of Jesus?

4. What do the teachings of Jesus mean to us today?

5. What is there about Jesus' teaching that speaks to us today?

6. How can we best live out the meaning of the teaching of Jesus?

7. What does every teacher, including Jesus, desire that his or her students do?

Close with a time of prayer, with each person praying for the ability to be students of Jesus who live his way and possibly teach his way.

"Behold The Man Who Trained Disciples"

In March of 1860 an ad appeared in many newspapers of the West. It read, "Wanted. Men, sturdy, young, not under 18, good riders, willing to face death. $25 per week. Orphans preferred." Many young men answered the call, and the Pony Express was born. A new chapter opened up in the history of this country.

A new chapter is always written in the life of the church whenever Christian people dare to reach out into some new frontier and carry the good news forward.

It was for this reason that Jesus chose disciples to follow him. So, as we think about Jesus moving always closer to Jerusalem — behold the man who trained disciples.

We know that very early in his ministry Jesus chose twelve to be disciples, learners, students. He trained them in the ways of the Kingdom, and prepared them to become the leaders of his church. He spoke to them those electrifying words, "Follow me." And they responded by going with him. Why was this so important?

James S. Stewart, the Scottish preacher, wrote in his book, *The Life And Teaching Of Jesus Christ*, about the purpose Jesus had in selecting disciples. He says the answer is found in Mark, chapter 3, where we read, "Then he appointed twelve, that they might be with him and that he might send them out to preach." Stewart says one reason is that they would be with him to learn, and the second is that they were to "carry and pass on the torch that Jesus had kindled."[1]

William Barclay points out that Jesus knew all along he would face a cross. He understood from the beginning that he must train disciples who would be "the living books on which he imprinted his message, the living instruments through whom his purposes could be carried out."[2]

We know that this training of the twelve was a vital part of the genius of that movement Jesus began. However, sometimes we overlook the fact that there were many other followers of Jesus. There were many disciples who were in that movement. The twelve disciples were the inner circle of trusted future leaders. They were closer to him than anyone else. They were with him more than anyone else.

The next group was what we call "the seventy." Our scripture passage relates their story. At one point, as Jesus began preparing to go to Jerusalem, the seventy were chosen for a special mission. No doubt Jesus had been training them also. Part of the Sermon on the Mount is teaching directed at his followers along with more general statements for the larger multitude. Perhaps at that point Jesus had already identified that special group of seventy, or at least had the idea in mind. We simply do not know all Jesus may have said to his followers. We have in the New Testament only a small part of what he said over three years. But we can assume Jesus put a great deal of time into training all of his disciples.

As Jesus was moving toward Jerusalem he planned to stop in several towns along the way. He had been in those towns before, but now he prepared the seventy to go on ahead and announce that he was coming that way. He told the seventy that the harvest was great, and that they should pray that

God would send out laborers into the harvest. Then he told them, "I am sending you out as lambs among wolves."

Now, sending them out was important not only on that occasion, but also it later became the same method the early church used in its mission to carry the gospel around the world. Jesus gave the twelve what we call "the great commission." He sent them out. That is the method Jesus used.

It is still the best method — sending out disciples to spread the good news about Jesus Christ, the Kingdom of God, the mission of the church of Christ. What if our church had seventy people, or seventeen, or even seven, who went out each week to invite others to come to this church and be a part of this fellowship? A new chapter would be written in the life of this church.

Let us take a closer look at what Jesus did with those seventy disciples.

*　*　*

The seventy were chosen. That is the first thing Luke tells us. He writes, "After these things the Lord appointed seventy others also." He chose them for this special mission. They were chosen to go prepare the way for him. They were to tell everyone that Jesus was coming that way. They were chosen for that purpose.

There was a reason Jesus did this. He told them, "The harvest is great, but the laborers are few; therefore pray the Lord of the harvest to send out laborers into his harvest." So, there was a great need for them to do this. Because of that need Jesus chose them.

All of us who are his disciples today have been chosen for such a purpose as this. We have been called to be disciples, servants, witnesses. All of these words imply action, movement, or doing something rather than being passive, standing still.

The Christian church has never been just a place for peaceful contemplation and thought. It has been throughout its history the largest volunteer group of activists in the world. From the beginning Jesus wanted it to be a group of laborers sent out into the harvest.

It is for this reason that we are involved in groups for study, learning and service. The church is a training school for Christian disciples.

We are trained for Christian living. We are trained to be people who make a difference in the world by the way we live, by our opinions, attitudes and convictions, and by the witness of our lives. We are trained to make a difference by the use of who we are and what we have, and to look at our resources, our talents and our money not as though we are obligated to give them, but as ways to serve and to support ministries of mercy throughout the world. We are trained to widen the Christian fellowship, and to bring others into our church, into groups within our church and under the influence of Christ. That is the kind of disciples we have been chosen to become. Is that what we are?

A farmer sold his land, moved into town, lost weight, bought a new wardrobe, had a facelift, bought a wig, and married a young widow. One day he was hit by a truck and killed. When he got to heaven he said to God, "Lord, why did you let this happen to me?" And God answered, "Why, George, I didn't even recognize you."

Would God recognize us? Are we what we have been chosen to become?

A man took his son off to college. They put all of his belongings in his room. Then they walked back out to the car. The man said to his son, "Don't you ever forget who you are."

We must remember who and what we have been chosen to become.

* * *

The sending was crucial. That is the second thing. Luke says Jesus "sent them out two by two before his face into every city and place where he himself was about to go." He told them everything to do. He told them to carry no money, pack or sandals. He also told them not to greet anyone on the road. Then he told them to go stay in the places which would receive them, and accept whatever the people gave them. They were to heal and preach, saying, "The Kingdom of God has come near." As people received or rejected them, so they received or rejected him.

So the sending was crucial. The sending out of the seventy was urgent. No time was to be lost. Their mission was of the utmost importance.

The mission of the church is always crucial.

A preacher went by to see one of the families in his church. Their youngest son answered the door. The preacher asked to see his parents, and learned they were not there. He then asked for a big brother or sister. The boy said, "They are not here, and I would not be here neither, but I've got the old tomcat in the freezer trying to turn him into a polar bear!" That was a crucial time in the old cat's life.

It is a crucial time in our world. This makes what we do in the church, with the church, for the church, as the church of utmost importance. We must not lose our sense of urgency.

David H. C. Read, a Presbyterian preacher in New York, preached a sermon in which he referred to what someone called "decaffeinated Christianity." It promises not to keep you awake at night.[3]

We must remember these are urgent times, and we must remember the urgency of our times is matched by the adequacy of our faith. Because that is true, the sending out of Christian disciples today is still crucial. Remember also that when we are sent just a few can accomplish so much. The influence of one Christian carries such an impact with it.

Jesus did not send all seventy disciples to the same place. He split them up and sent them two by two. Sometimes it only takes a few. Such a great difference can be made by the influence of one life over another.

In a group discussion about the influence of others, one young lady told of her family having Elton Trueblood stay in their home when she was about ten years old. The great Quaker teacher, preacher and writer was speaking in their town for several days. During mealtime they would talk, and he would ask the adults questions. After listening to them he would ask her the same question, and then listen to what she said. She told the group, "He treated me as if I were an intelligent, sensitive, mature Christian. And, that week I made up my mind that I was going to spend the rest of my life becoming one."[4]

You can have the same influence on the lives of other people. It is crucial that we do that.

* * *

Finally, the success was certain. That is the third thing. Luke writes, "Then the servants returned with joy, saying, 'Lord, even the demons are subject to us in your name.' " They had been sent out by Jesus to prepare the way for him, to preach the Kingdom of God, and to heal the sick, and when they returned they were amazed at what they had been able to do. Jesus responded by saying, "I saw Satan fall like lightning from heaven. Behold I give you authority to trample on serpents and scorpions, and over all the power of the enemy, and nothing shall by any means hurt you. Nevertheless do not rejoice in this, that the spirits are subject to you, but rather rejoice because your names are written in heaven."

When we use the method of Jesus our success is certain. A difference is made in the lives of other people, in our lives, in the life of the church, in the life of our community.

That same kind of success is certain when we remember who we serve.

David Livingston said of his missionary journeys in Africa, "Jesus and I went through the jungles together." That is who we serve.

That same kind of success is certain when we remember the nature of our service. We cannot do everything. But we can do something.

William H. Willimon told of a man who said, "A good teacher must be content to be a sower rather than a reaper." He went on to say teachers do not see good results immediately. The good they do shows up later on.[5]

That same kind of success is certain when we remember the importance of caring.

A businessman ran an ad in the paper which was printed wrong. It read, "We fake a personal interest in each one." The world has had enough of that. All around people are crying out for someone who cares, who takes a personal interest.

That same kind of success is certain when we remember the impact and influence of our own lives. It is the old story of actions speaking louder than words, and living the things we say we believe.

That is always the key, is it not? The question for us always is whether or not we will allow ourselves to become trained disciples who are chosen, who are sent, who are successful.

A small town doctor learned of a woman who was gravely ill. She lived alone, shut off from the better people in town. The doctor let it be known that no Christian should let a situation like hers go unattended. The pastor of one of the churches told her story on a Sunday night after he had just learned about her. The next morning he went to the woman's house, and found it was not like the doctor had described. The house was cleaned up. The floors were still damp from mopping. Groceries had been brought in. Clothes were being washed. The preacher found the wealthiest woman in his church doing all this. He said to her, "Oh, you shouldn't be out here doing all this. Why didn't you just send your maid?" She replied, "That is the trouble with so much of our religion. So often we send someone else. This time I just decided to go myself. I thought if I did maybe this lady would be able to meet Jesus."[6]

There are many times here in our community when if anyone is to meet Jesus at all it will be not because we sent somebody else, but because he sent you.

1. James S. Stewart, *The Life And Teaching Of Jesus Christ,* Abingdon Press, Nashville, 1957, p. 68.

2. William Barclay, *The Mind Of Jesus,* Harper & Row Publisher, New York and Evanston, 1960, p. 61.

3. David H. C. Read, "When We Say: 'No One Is Perfect,' " *Pulpit Digest,* January/February 1992, p. 33.

4. Richard A. Hasler, *Emphasis,* CSS Publishing Co., Lima, Ohio, September-October, 1992, p. 44.

5. William H. Willimon, *Clergy and Laity Burnout,* Abingdon Press, Nashville, 1989, p. 32.

6. T. Cecil Myers, "On Letting The Soul Catch Up With The Body," February 14, 1982, (an unpublished sermon).

Our Father and our God, in whom we find life, we gather to worship thee that we may continue to have life and have it more abundantly.

We thank thee for the gift of thy Son and his life in this world. We are thankful for the call to be his disciples, and on these Sundays in Lent we are especially in tune with the words, "Follow me." Enable us to follow him and give our lives to him.

Help us, Father, to know what it means to be disciples. Call us to greater service in thy Kingdom.

Equip us with all the faith, courage, and hope we need. Give us a great vision by which we may serve and live.

May we learn to see our challenges as opportunities, our problems as possibilities, our disappointments as his appointments.

Forgive our sins. Take away our cowardice. Remove our self-centeredness. Mold us into the likeness of thy Son.

Bless us as a church with vision and imagination. Help us to see all we can become, understand all we need, know all we can accomplish, and serve in all the ways we can all the people we can.

Bless our sick and sorrowful. Teach them, and be the great physician for them. Comfort those who mourn.

Bless the leaders of the world with wisdom and good sense, mercy and compassion and a concern for the well-being of people the world over.

We make this our prayer in Jesus' name. Amen.

"It's Spring Training Time"
Object: a newspaper sports page

Good morning, boys and girls. I am so glad you are here today for Sunday school and church. Today is the Fourth Sunday in Lent. As we continue to think about Jesus on the way to Jerusalem, I want us to look at the way he trained his disciples.

Look at this. It's the sports page from a recent newspaper. This paper has in it some reports from spring training. Who can tell us what spring training is? That is right. This is a time when all the big league baseball teams go to Florida or Arizona to get ready for the new season. They train, or practice, and try to improve and learn new things about playing. They get their bodies into good shape.

Most everything we do requires some training. Whatever we choose to do in life, whether it is playing ball, playing the piano, singing, dancing, or whatever, always involves a time of training, study, and practice.

Jesus knew this was important for his disciples as well. He called many people to follow him. There were the twelve disciples and also another group of seventy, as we will read about from the Bible today. Jesus trained all of these people in what it meant to follow him and love and serve God.

Now, you see, this is what we do here in our church each Sunday as we come to Sunday school and church. We are learning how to be followers of Jesus. We are learning how to be Christians. It takes a long time to learn all this. We will be learning this all of our lives. So, come every Sunday as we learn together.

May we pray. Father, help us to learn more about you and how you want us to live. Amen.

Prelude

Chiming Of The Hour

Introit

The Hymn Of Praise "Jesus, Keep Me Near The Cross"

Affirmation Of Faith   The Apostles' Creed

Invocation

Moments Of Fellowship

Pastoral Prayer And The Lord's Prayer

The Children's Message "It's Spring Training Time"

The Anthem "When I Survey The Wondrous Cross"

The Prayer Of Dedication

The Offertory

The Doxology

The Hymn Of Preparation "He Leadeth Me, O Blessed
    Thought"

Scripture Lesson Luke 10:1-20

Sermon "Behold The Man Who Trained Disciples"

Invitation To Christian Discipleship

Hymn Of Invitation "Were You There?"

Benediction

The Choral Response

Postlude

1. Have someone read the scripture lesson again: Luke 10:1-20.

2. Ask several in the group to share what this passage means to them.

3. In what ways do you feel God has called you to serve him?

4. How might the average person in a church live out the meaning of discipleship?

5. When do we know we are being "successful" as disciples?

6. How can we gain new disciples for Christ in our own churches?

7. What might God be calling your church to do as an expression of a deeper discipleship?

Close with sentence prayers centered on the desire for a deeper discipleship. Have someone pray a closing prayer.

"Behold The Man Who Turned Toward Jerusalem"

Some time ago I was reading Harold Kushner's book, *Who Needs God.* I was struck by a story he told in that book. He said he was talking with a nurse once who related a conversation she had with a young lady. This young lady's boyfriend was dying of cancer. The nurse asked her if she could do anything for her. The young lady answered, "Yeah, remind me never to love anybody this much again."[1]

Now we come to that part of Christ's story where Jesus begins to look toward the cross. There is a difference now in the atmosphere. There is an underlying tension as Jesus begins to move away from peaceful Galilee and toward tense, up-tight Jerusalem.

In his telling of this story Luke at this point relates, "He steadfastly set his face to go to Jerusalem."

I cannot help but wonder if the disciples had at this point realized what would happen when they got to Jerusalem, would they have finished the trip? Perhaps they would be saying to each other, "Remind me never to love anybody this much again."

I read again in a church bulletin something I had heard years ago, but had forgotten. It is said the Chinese have a word which has two meanings. It means "crisis." That is the first meaning. But it also means "opportunity." Going to Jerusalem was certainly a crisis. It was also an opportunity. Jesus knew he had to do it. It was out of that crisis situation that his Father would find such an opportunity. Behold the man who turned toward Jerusalem.

There finally came a day when Jesus was faced with a great decision. There were two roads lying before him, and he had to choose one of them. He knew that if he chose the road to Jerusalem he would be on a road headed to a destination from which there would be no return. In fact, it was a choice he had already been making all along. But finally there came a time for him to make it known and head that way.

Now here they were traveling along that road which would take them to Jerusalem. Mark tells us that Jesus was walking out ahead of the twelve disciples. They were lagging back a little, taking uncertain steps. Mark tells us, "They were afraid." At that point Jesus gathered them closer to him and said to them, "Behold, we are going up to Jerusalem, and the Son of Man will be delivered to the chief priests and to the scribes, and they will condemn him to death and deliver him to the Gentiles; and they will mock him, and scourge him, and spit on him, and kill him. And the third day he will rise again."

Yes, Jesus turned toward Jerusalem. He set out on that road which would take him to the heart of that city, down its main street, into the upper room, out to the garden, into the palace, and out to a hill they called the place of the skull.

Jesus knew in his heart where he was headed. He also knew this was the thing for him to do. This is what he had been born to do. This was the hour for which he had been living. This was the purpose for which his father sent him into the world. And, this is what would make him who he is in our eyes today.

Garibaldi, the Italian patriot, once said, "It is the big demand that makes the heroic spirit. It is the big demand that makes the big soul."[2]

Jesus turned toward Jerusalem where he faced the big demand which awaited him there. As we think about this, perhaps if we look closer at it we will see better the choices which are always before us.

* * *

Jesus chose not the road of selfishness but the road of sacrifice. The road to Jerusalem was the road of sacrifice. The temple in Jerusalem was the place of sacrifice for the Jewish people. It had been that way for a long time. But this time there was something different. This time Jesus himself would be the sacrifice. And so he said to the twelve, "Behold, we are going up to Jerusalem, and the Son of Man will be delivered to the chief priests and to the scribes."

It would have been so easy for Jesus to travel the selfish road. He could have used his power and ability for selfish ends. He could have raised an army and gathered the masses around himself, marched right into Jerusalem and become the King of the Jews. After all, this is probably what many people wanted him to do anyway. But he turned away from all of that, and turned toward Jerusalem, the place of sacrifice.

He went there unarmed, backed not by an army of force, but an army of love, an army made up of simple folk, women and children. He went there not to wage war, but to surrender. He went there not to gain a momentous victory, but to suffer a momentary defeat. He chose not to gain the spoils of war, but to give himself away.

Through what Jesus did he instilled that same spirit of sacrifice in his disciples. They would choose later to live the same way. Their lives were transformed by him, and they also became self-giving people.

This spirit of sacrifice has always characterized Christian people at their best. Christian people at their best are also sacrificial people. They catch that same spirit, and they give themselves away.

That choice is a constant one before us. We face it always. We come to so many turns in the road where we have to decide if we will live for ourselves only, or if we will instead live for something greater than we are, something grand and beautiful.

This great need for people who sacrifice is built into the way things are. Nothing important is ever gained without it. The Kingdom of God still needs people who are willing to give themselves away.

It is true that we take a chance when we do that. These days we have become cynical to the point of not trusting many people.

Henry Ford was on a vacation trip to Ireland. While he was there he was asked to make a contribution to an orphanage. He wrote out a check for $5,000. The next day headlines in the paper read, "Henry Ford Gives Orphanage $50,000." Later that day the director of the orphanage called and apologized. Henry Ford said, "Never mind. I'm giving you a check for the other $45,000, but only under one condition. When the new building goes up I want this inscription over the door, 'I was a stranger and you took me in.' "

Even though we know there are many people in our world today who are takers we are still called by God to be givers.

What would have happened if Jesus had not given himself? What if the disciples had not done that? What if you and I no longer did that? The Christian church would cease to exist and God would have no witness in his world. The world has enough selfish people already. What the world needs is Kingdom of God people who give themselves.

Some years ago in Russia a group of Christians were meeting secretly one night. Suddenly, two Russian army officers burst into their meeting. They said to the people, "Leave immediately or we will kill you." A few of the Christians left, but the others remained. The two officers locked the door. Then they turned around and said, "We are Christians, too. We just did not want to be with anyone not willing to pay the price."

The question is always whether we are willing to pay the price, and travel the road of sacrifice.

* * *

Jesus chose not the road of safety but the road of suffering. The road to Jerusalem was the road of suffering. That is where it led. Jesus knew all along that is what it meant. That is why he also said to the disciples, "And they will condemn him to death and deliver him to the Gentiles; and they will mock him, and scourge him, and spit on him, and kill him."

The road of safety is such an easy road to travel. It is the road which winds and wanders endlessly with no direction to it. It is the road of least resistance. It is the road which does not offend, never protests, never objects. It is the road cowards travel.

This is not the road Jesus chose. He took the road which led to Golgotha, the place of the skull, the execution site for the city of Jerusalem. It was the way of the cross.

He told his disciples that if they were going to follow him they need not expect anything any different. There would be a cross out there for them on some future lonely road or some hill of one kind or another.

If we are true to our Lord we cannot choose the road of safety either. We cannot travel the road of easy living and unconcerned attitudes. We cannot take the road of token involvement. We cannot keep Christ and the church and the world and each other all at a safe distance. We cannot protect ourselves from doing too much, giving too much and becoming too involved in the church simply because we have other things to do, and we want to keep on living our private lives.

We will never understand, appreciate, or live the Christian life if our main concern is our own safety. We simply have to give ourselves to the cause of the Kingdom of God with complete abandon. It will not work any other way. To travel the road Jesus chose is not easy. But, the important things never are easy. There is always a burden to bear.

When John F. Kennedy was President he often became so discouraged he wanted to give the job to Lyndon Johnson. When Lyndon Johnson finally got the job he often wanted to give it to Hubert Humphrey. Hubert Humphrey said his greatest honor was being nominated for President by his party, and his greatest disappointment was losing the race.

The Christian life is not a life of ease and safety. It involves suffering, our own suffering, and taking upon ourselves the suffering of others. It means bearing the world's hurts and problems. Obviously that is more than we can do on our own. The good news is we are not on our own.

Carl Michalson, in his book *Faith For Personal Crises*, told the story of Felicitas of Carthage. She was a Christian who was persecuted and placed in prison. While there she had a baby. When she cried out in pain, she was asked how she would be able to endure her death by beasts. She replied, "Now I suffer what I suffer; then another will be in me who will suffer for me, as I shall suffer for him."[3]

In one of his sermons Phillips Brooks said, "O, do not pray for easy lives. Pray to be stronger men! Do not pray for tasks equal to your powers. Pray for powers equal to your tasks! Then the doing of your work shall not be a miracle. But you shall be a miracle. Every day you shall wonder at yourself, at the richness of life which has come to you by the grace of God."

The greatest miracle of the New Testament is not that Jesus gave sight to the blind and made the lame to walk. It is that he gives sight to us who can already see and walks with us on the road to the crosses he gives us to bear for him.

*   *   *

Finally, Jesus chose not the road of security but the road of service. The road to Jerusalem was the road of service. That is what it meant. Jesus knew all along this is what he was doing. He was serving his Father and through what would happen he would be serving all the world. That is why he could say about all he would endure, "And the third day he will rise again." He knew that was the hope of the world. That was why he had said, "I came not to be served, but to serve, and to give my life as a ransom for many." He was not afraid to take the risk. He was not looking for security. He wanted only to serve.

Not only was this true for him, but also it was true for all who would follow him. He reminded his disciples when two of them asked for a place of glory that "whoever would be great among you must be your servant, and whoever would be first among you must be your slave." This way of service was the only way which led to the things Jesus was trying to accomplish. He wanted his followers to know they must travel in this same way.

Here is one of the great secrets of the Christian life. The real joy of living comes to us when we have given ourselves in service to the Kingdom of God. It comes to us when we give ourselves with the same devotion Jesus had as he gave himself. So, you see, the cross is not only that place where we see God's love expressed and find new life, it is also where we hear the call to service.

Two little girls were at the movies one afternoon. It was a film on the life of Jesus. They watched it until that scene where Jesus was being crucified. Then one punched the other and said, "Let's go. This is the place where we came in."

At one point Jesus said only those willing to take up the cross would be fit to follow him.

The cross becomes real for us when we begin not only to see that Jesus died for us there, but also when we hear in that the call to serve him. He calls us to choose the way of the cross.

One year we put up three crosses for our sunrise service. They were still up for a few days the next week. One afternoon I saw three boys come through our yard. They stopped and looked at those crosses. They seemed to be talking about them. Then one of the boys stepped over to the one in the middle, stood in front of it, stretched out his arms and showed the other two how it was done.

That is what Jesus did. He shows us how to take up the cross. And he calls us to meet him on the way to the cross — the way that leads to life. Will you meet him there and become a follower of the way of the cross?

---

1. Harold Kushner, *Who Needs God,* Summit Books, New York, 1989, p. 28.

2. Charles L. Wallis, Editor, *A Treasury Of Sermon Illustrations,* Abingdon-Cokesbury Press, New York-Nashville, 1950, p. 165.

3. Carl Michalson, *Faith For Personal Crises,* Charles Scribner's Sons, New York, 1959, p. 151.

Our Father, as we gather to worship thee may our songs and prayers bring glory to thee, for we have gathered to worship and serve thee and to give ourselves to thee.

We are thankful, O God, for all thy blessings upon us, for we have seen thy hands at work in our lives. We know we have been blessed abundantly by thee, and we are thankful for all good gifts we have received out of thy goodness.

We are thankful for the great decisions made by thy Son Jesus Christ. We think of him today turning his face toward Jerusalem, and being willing to go there and face the cross for us and because of us.

We pray today that we would be able to have the same steadfast devotion to thy Kingdom. Help us to be people of courage and dedication. Enable us to be tough-minded and centered in thee and thy will.

Because we have answered the call to thy people, put within each of us the faith, hope and courage we need to serve thee and to be the church of Christ.

Lead us to give ourselves to thee more completely, to see thee more clearly, to love thee more dearly, and to follow thee more nearly day by day.

Make us more loving, more understanding, and more compassionate, and enable us to be gentle, kind, courageous, brave and bold.

Bless those of our church and community who are sick and in sorrow. Bless people the world over who suffer. Help us help them, in Jesus' name we pray. Amen.

"Marching Off The Map"
Object: a map of the Holy Land

Good morning, boys and girls. I hope all of you are doing well today. Thanks for being here this morning. I am glad to see you. This is the Fifth Sunday in the season of Lent. We are thinking together about Jesus going to Jerusalem.

Today I want to show you a map. This is a map of the Holy Land, where Jesus lived along with all the people we read about in the Bible. In a minute I want to show you some things on this map.

First, I want to tell you a story. When Columbus and other explorers set out to find new trade routes to the far east they had no maps. It was because of that fact that Columbus, on the way to India, discovered America. In a sense he sailed off the maps they had. As a result they drew new maps.

Now, look at this map of the Holy Land. Jesus lived up here in Nazareth until he was 30 years old. When he began his ministry he moved over here to a city on the Sea of Galilee called Capernaum. He lived here for three years. Then he traveled down the Jordan valley and came up a long road to Jerusalem. There we know he was crucified, dead and buried.

Today in our Bible reading we are hearing about Jesus making the decision to do that. In some ways he was deciding to march right off the map. He was doing something no one else had done. But he knew God would be with him and lead him through all he would face as he went to the cross and the tomb. He knew God would raise him up from the dead. In that, he has found the way for us to new life in the resurrection. He has drawn with his life a new map for us.

May we pray. O God, help us to be brave like Jesus and follow where you lead us. In his name we pray. Amen.

Prelude

Chiming Of The Hour

Introit

The Hymn Of Praise "In The Cross Of Christ I Glory"

Affirmation Of Faith   The Apostles' Creed

Invocation

Moments Of Fellowship

Pastoral Prayer And The Lord's Prayer

The Children's Message "Marching Off The Map"

The Anthem "The People Of God"

The Prayer Of Dedication

The Offertory

The Doxology

The Hymn Of Preparation "Soldiers Of Christ, Arise"

Scripture Lesson Mark 10:32-34

Sermon "Behold The Man Who Turned Toward Jerusalem"

Invitation To Christian Discipleship

Hymn Of Invitation "Ah, Holy Jesus"

Benediction

The Choral Response

Postlude

1. Have someone read the scripture lesson: Mark 10:32-34. Let several describe what this turning meant.

2. Why did Jesus have to do this?

3. Why was this difficult for the disciples to accept and understand?

4. Have you faced such times of decision in your own life?

5. What enabled you to face these times and overcome them?

6. What do we learn in times of difficulty and suffering?

7. Where do we find the inner resources for living through times of difficulty?

Have someone prepared in advance to lead the group in Saint Augustine's serenity prayer, and then close with a prayer of benediction.

"Behold The Man Who Tried To Be King"

Some time ago there was a stage play called *Construction*. It was the story of some people who wanted to build a wall. But there was a young man there who urged them instead to build a bridge. The people turned on him and killed him because of what he wanted them to do. After they killed him one of the characters said, "We can't go on crucifying the truth forever."[1]

When Jesus went to Jerusalem he found a wall. He had come to build a bridge. But he knew all along that on the other side of the wall his crucifixion awaited him.

One of the hotels where we have stayed in Jerusalem is located on the Mount of Olives. You can look back behind that hotel toward Bethany and Bethphage. Standing out in front of that hotel you can look over the wall into the old city of Jerusalem. Usually a man is there who offers camel rides. It is a really good deal. It costs only one dollar to get on a camel for a ride. It costs ten dollars to get off. I was going to take a picture of that old camel while he was lying down taking a nap. Just as I snapped it a boy on a donkey rode right in front of me. He is all you see in the picture.

I thought of another one riding a donkey across that mountain just up from where I was standing. The bustling city was there waiting on him. Down the Mount of Olives he rode, across the Kidron Valley, then up the hill toward the gates of the city.

What a striking sight it must have been! Jesus knew, as everyone else knew, what it meant for him to enter Jerusalem like this. The old kings had always come into the city to begin their rule in this way, riding on a donkey. It was a lowly animal signifying peace. The people would line the road waving palm branches and calling out, "Hosanna! Blessed is he who comes in the name of the Lord! Hosanna in the highest!"

Jesus knew what he was doing. He knew what it meant. He knew what those people in Jerusalem would think when they saw him coming to town this way.

Today on this Palm Sunday — behold the man who tried to be king.

As we think about this today let us be clear in our understanding, and remind ourselves that in many ways Palm Sunday was a mockery. Even though thousands waved palm branches with their hands, for so many of them their hearts were not in it. Even though Jesus was trying to be king, for so many of those people he did not look like a king, did not act like a king, and would not be crowned as a king by them. They knew what they wanted, and they knew what Jesus said and did was not it.

They wanted a great kingdom of glory, but Jesus said, "The Kingdom of God is within you."

They wanted a restoration of their former power and wealth, but Jesus said, "The Kingdom of God is like a grain of mustard seed."

They wanted a display of majesty and honor, but Jesus said, "The Kingdom of God is like a seed growing secretly. No one sees it or knows it is there."

They wanted their freedom from the bondage of Rome, but Jesus said, "You shall know the truth and the truth shall make you free." And later he said, "I am the way, and the truth, and the life."

Yet, even though Jerusalem accepted him only during the parade, there were many in the crowd that day who had come down from Galilee for the Passover season. They knew who Jesus was, and many of them were loyal to him. They knew and accepted the meaning of his entrance into the city.

James Stewart, the Scottish preacher, said that as Jesus went to the capital city "he openly accepted the tribute" of the crowd, and in entering Jerusalem as a king he was acting out a living parable about who he was.[2]

We think about this today. But let me remind us also that Palm Sunday is still before us today. It will not let us rest. It will not let us go. It will not turn us loose or let us turn aside. Palm Sunday and all of its choices still confront us today.

So on this Palm Sunday, behold the man who tried to be king, and understand these things about him.

* * *

His fame was easily gained. Everyone knew he was coming to Jerusalem. We are told that "a great multitude spread their garments on the road; others cut down branches from the trees and spread them on the road." Soon the whole city of Jerusalem was aware of what was going on. And they all turned out to see him.

Jesus was in the limelight that day. He was the object of everyone's attention. Everyone wanted to see the parade. Jesus had no trouble drawing a crowd that day. His fame was easily gained.

It had been that way for Jesus all throughout his ministry in Galilee. Everywhere he went great crowds of people came to hear him. They sought him out. It was said of him, "The common people heard him gladly." Up in Galilee on several occasions thousands of people came out from the towns to hear him preach on the side of a mountain. His fame spread throughout all of Galilee and beyond. When he came down to Jericho, the people there knew of him and turned out to see him off on his way up to Jerusalem.

This happened because of who he was, the words he spoke, the things he did, and what he meant to people.

It was the message, the good news about all of this and his death and resurrection that caused his fame to spread and faith in him to spread out all over the Roman world in a very short time. Now, he is known, honored, worshipped, and served all over the world.

A bishop was visiting a church one Sunday, and he was talking with a little boy. He said, "Son, I'll give you an orange if you can tell me where God is." The boy said, "I'll give you two if you can tell me where he is not."[3]

You cannot name a place where Jesus is not known, loved and served. We serve him today and gather in his name. But we must remember that sometimes our attachments can be weak, our commitments shallow, and our interest fleeting.

Archbishop William Temple was staying in someone's home overnight. He was about to go down for breakfast when he heard the lady of the house singing "Nearer My God To Thee." He thought about that woman's faith and commitment beginning the day that way. When he got to the kitchen he said something to her about it, and she answered, "Oh, yes. That's the hymn I use for boiling eggs — three verses for soft-boiled and five for hard-boiled."[4]

It turned out to be a shallow kind of faith. That is the faith many had in Jesus when his fame was easily gained.

* * *

We also need to understand that allegiance to Jesus costs nothing. Watching the parade that day did not require anything. Multitudes of people turned out to see Jesus. Many of those bystanders joined in with those who went before and those who followed after shouting, "Hosanna! Blessed is he who comes in the name of the Lord! Hosanna in the highest!" But, you see, those people in the crowd that day were not required to do anything costly. All they had to do was stand there and shout and watch the parade go by. They did not even have to shout. Many of them were there simply because they were curious. They just wanted to find out what was going on. Allegiance to him cost nothing.

However, all along the way Jesus had been saying it does cost something. It costs everything. So it was that he said, "If any man would come after me let him deny himself, take up the cross and follow me. He who tries to save his life will lose it, but he who loses his life for my sake will find it. No one can serve two masters for he will hate the one and love the other."

Like the crowd in Jerusalem on that first Palm Sunday we could easily think allegiance to him costs nothing. That leads us to crown him king only for a day, fleeting moments here and there which require of us absolutely nothing.

Dietrich Bonhoeffer said in his book, *The Cost Of Discipleship,* that "cheap grace is the deadly enemy of our church." It requires no repentance, no discipleship, no confession. It is "grace without the cross."³ Without that there is no Jesus, no king, no kingdom.

Still today we are called to be disciples who follow, who serve, who give ourselves, who live the abundant life and share it with the world.

One year at Annual Conference when our retiring ministers were being recognized, the Bishop told about the wife of one of them. He told of what a dynamic person she was and how she was full of life, deeply concerned about her fellowman. One day she was walking down a street in downtown Atlanta. She saw a man lying on the sidewalk, face down. She thought, "Oh, no! He's dying." Quickly she reviewed the lifesaving steps she had learned in a CPR class. She rushed over to him, rolled him over, threw his head back, held his nose and began giving him the breath of life. But he fought her, kicked and flung his arms around. She said, "Man, what's wrong with you?" He replied, "Lady, I work for the phone company. I was just checking out this circuit box under the sidewalk."

Maybe sometimes we get carried away. But I would rather that someone be too anxious to do something than not enough

— too committed than not enough — too willing than not enough — wanting to do too much rather than nothing.

Many of those people who saw Jesus that day wanted to do nothing, and that cost them nothing.

* * *

Finally, his popularity soon faded. The parade came to an end when Jesus got there. When he arrived in Jerusalem, "All the city was moved saying, 'Who is this?' " His supporters answered, "This is Jesus, the prophet from Nazareth." Then Jesus went immediately into the Temple. He drove out the moneychangers who were cheating people as they exchanged their money for temple-money. From Sunday it was all downhill the rest of the week. His popularity soon faded.

People began to understand what Jesus was saying and who he was. The people in Jerusalem, with the help of the Pharisees and the priests, began to turn against him. Jesus simply could not do the things he did, say the things he said, and be the person he was and get away with it.

Years ago there was a television program called *Truth Or Consequences*. When our daughter Sheri was about seven or eight, she came in the den one night just as the news was going off and that program was coming on. She said, "Hey, what's on — the Consequences Of Telling The Truth?"

Jesus would face them that week. People began to understand him. When that happened the political leaders began to reject his concept of the kingdom for he spoke of the Kingdom of God. The religious authorities rejected his plan of salvation for he spoke about a change of heart. The disciples fell away from their discipleship, the thrill of Palm Sunday passed and they saw the cross staring Jesus in the face. The people of Jerusalem called him King on Sunday, and by Friday they gave him a crown of thorns. They were willing to place him on a throne on his first day, and five days later they placed him on a cross. The throng gave him thorns instead of a throne.

They pluck their palm branches and
hail Him as King early on Sunday.
They spread out their garments;
Hosannas they sing early on Sunday.
But, where is the noise of their hurrying feet,
the crown they would offer, the scepter, the seat?
Their King wanders hungry, forgot on the street,
early on Monday.[6]

But, what about this Palm Sunday? Let us take this whole story out of the past and bring it up to date. Let us pretend word has gotten out that Jesus is coming to our town. And let us pretend we all go out in front of this church and stand there by the side of the street waving our palm branches with shouts of "Hosanna."

What are we doing? Are we really making Jesus our King, or merely King for a day? Are we just watching the parade, or are we really giving ourselves to him? You are the crowd on this Palm Sunday, and you must decide.

Later in the week they took Jesus before the Roman governor, Pontius Pilate. He said to the people, "Behold the man!" They cried out for the crucifixion of Jesus. Pilate examined him again, still finding no fault in him. The people said, "Whoever makes himself a king speaks against Caesar." Pilate sat in the judgment seat and said, "Behold your king!" When the people responded with "Crucify him!" Pilate then asked, "Shall I crucify your King?" The chief priests answered, "We have no king but Caesar!"

What about this Palm Sunday? Who is your king? "Behold the man. What shall I do with Jesus?" still is the question.

There was a woman who lived a good life, spending most of her days in comfort and ease. In her final years she was confined to her bed in a nursing home. Her resources were gone. Her existence was meager. She knew she was dying, and one day she said to her pastor, "I want someone to sing 'I'm The Child Of A King' at my funeral." All of us can be if we choose to be.

There was a play about the life of Emily Dickinson. Julie Harris portrayed her. At one point she talks about religion and says, "I do believe that no person can be truly happy until that person can say, 'I love Christ.' "[7]

Palm Sunday confronts us with the necessity of making a choice about just that. What about it on this Palm Sunday?

---

1. James W. Moore, *Yes Lord I Have Sinned,* Abingdon Press, Nashville, 1991, p. 70.

2. James S. Stewart, *The Life And Teaching Of Jesus Christ,* Abingdon Press, Nashville, 1957, p. 182.

3. Hugh H. Drennan, *Emphasis,* CSS Publishing Co., Lima, Ohio. September-October, 1992, p. 55.

4. Robert W. Spain, *How To Stay Alive As Long As You Live,* Dimensions For Living, Nashville, 1992, p. 135.

5. Wallace W. Kirby, *Emphasis, op. cit.,* p. 15.

6. Edwin McNeill Poteat, "Palm Sunday And Monday," *Over The Sea, The Sky,* Harper & Brothers, New York, 1945, p. 126.

7. Edward W. Bauman, *God's Presence In My Life,* Abingdon, Nashville, 1981, p. 23.

Eternal God and Father of all, we enter thy gates with thanksgiving and come into thy courts with praise. As we bow down before thee, accept the worship and allegiance we offer to thee and thy Kingdom.

On this Palm Sunday, O God, we remember how Jesus entered Jerusalem, and we join the unending hymn, "Hosanna in the highest. Blessed is he who comes in the name of the Lord." We remember today that he went there for all of us. We are thankful, Father, for him, and we know it is because of him that we may live lives of victory and hope. We are thankful for his courage as it led him to face the cross, though it brought suffering to him. His courage combined with thy good will has brought new life to all the earth.

Because of this, we can thank thee for our own times of suffering, though they bring us much anguish, because we know thy love and good will are at work for us even as they were for thy Son. And because of that, we will find our way.

Help us, O God, to be people of steadfast and stalwart faith that we may not be victimized by our circumstances, but the victors over them, even as Jesus was victorious over the cross.

Forgive our sins and enable us to know thy will and do it, for it is in this way that we will do well and thy Kingdom will come for us.

Touch the sick and sorrowful of our church and community and those who suffer everywhere. We pray in Jesus' name. Amen.

"Wave The Flag"
Object: a flag and a palm branch

Good morning, boys and girls. Isn't it great to be here on Palm Sunday? I am so glad you came today, and that all of you were able to come in with the choir and wave your palm branches. You did a really good job with that. Today on Palm Sunday we think about Jesus entering Jerusalem. When he did that everyone in town came out to see him.

You know, they say everyone loves a parade. When we go to a parade, we like to wave the flag. See this flag. At parades many people have them, and some carry large flags.

When Jesus came into Jerusalem it was a big parade because some were calling him the new king of the Jews. They were welcoming him into the city. Of course, they did not wave flags like ours. What they waved were palm branches like this palm branch and the ones you brought in today. That was an old custom among those people. It was the way they always received a new king. But we know they did not really mean it, most of them, because they turned against Jesus and refused to let him be the king of their lives.

Today Palm Sunday means for us that we want Jesus to be the king of our lives. We want him to live in us and help us. We want to love him and serve him. We want to belong to him and live for him.

Think about this today. Let Jesus be your king and welcome him into your life, and all of your plans and hopes and dreams for the future.

May we pray. Help us, Father, to open up our lives that the king of glory may come in and live in us. Amen.

Prelude

Chiming Of The Hour

Introit

The Hymn Of Praise "All Glory, Laud And Honor"

Affirmation Of Faith   The Apostles' Creed

Invocation

Moments Of Fellowship

Pastoral Prayer And The Lord's Prayer

The Children's Message "Wave The Flag"

The Anthem "Lift Up Your Heads"

The Prayer Of Dedication

The Offertory

The Doxology

The Hymn Of Preparation "Hosanna, Loud Hosanna"

Scripture Lesson Matthew 21:1-10

Sermon "Behold The Man Who Tried To Be King"

Invitation To Christian Discipleship

Hymn Of Invitation "Rejoice, Ye Pure In Heart"

Benediction

The Choral Response

Postlude

1. Have someone again read the scripture lesson: Matthew 21:1-10.

2. Let several people share what they think the situation in Jerusalem was like as Jesus came to the city.

3. What was the significance of Jesus entering the city riding on a donkey?

4. How did the people in Jerusalem react to Jesus' entry?

5. What does Palm Sunday mean to you today?

6. How might we open our lives to the coming of the King?

7. How can we let Jesus rule our lives?

In closing have someone read Psalm 22. Then, end with sentence prayers.

Easter Sunday Sermon
Luke 24:36-43

"Behold The Man Who Took The Victory"

One Sunday a man was riding a subway in New York. Suddenly another man and his children got on the subway. They were making all kinds of noise, yelling, throwing things, and running around the car. What had been a peaceful group of people reading their papers and minding their own business was interrupted by all this madness. The father of these children had sat down by this other man who was already on the subway. Finally, this man told the father that his children were bothering a lot of people. The father replied, "Oh, you're right. I guess I should do something about it. We just came from the hospital where their mother died about an hour ago. I don't know what to think, and I guess they don't know how to handle it either."[1]

That describes so well the shape the disciples were in from Friday afternoon all the way up to Sunday morning. They were at a complete loss. Everything they had bet their lives on over the last three years had come tumbling in around them. They had pinned all their hopes on Jesus, and they saw Jesus defeated. But then the morning came, and the morning brought

81

the light of a new day. Since that morning nothing has ever been the same.

On this Easter Sunday morning — behold the man who took the victory.

All Jesus of Nazareth was, all he said, all he represented, all he came to do was focused toward this moment. The resurrection of Jesus is his defining moment. More than anything else he said, or did, or accomplished, this made him who he is in the eyes of the world, in the eyes of his enemies, in the eyes of his followers, and in the eyes of untold millions of people across 20 centuries. This was his defining moment, and this enables us to see who he is.

In one of his books United Methodist minister Dr. Charles Allen quotes a historian who wrote, "When the final history of mankind has been written, its proudest glory would be that there once walked into ancient Jerusalem and into the hearts of mankind a simple peasant named Jesus of Nazareth."[2]

Because of him and because of what happened in the early morning of a spring day in old Jerusalem the entire world and the history of humankind has never been the same.

We remember the story well. It was early that morning that the women went out to the garden tomb. They intended to anoint the body of Jesus with spices. But when they arrived, no one was there. As they wondered about what this meant, the angel of the Lord said to them, "Why do you seek the living among the dead? He is not here but is risen."

The women went immediately to tell the disciples. The disciples came running out to the tomb, and they also found it was empty. They all began to realize the things Jesus had told them were true.

We are not sure how they spent that day, but Luke and John both tell us that late in the evening they were all together in the upper room. Mark simply writes, "afterward." Suddenly Jesus came into the room where they were. He said to them, "Peace to you." Sensing they were afraid, he said, "Why are you troubled? Why do doubts arise in your hearts? Behold in my hands and my feet, that it is I myself. Handle me and see, for a spirit does not have flesh and bones as you see I have." Then he shared a meal with them.

Nothing has ever been the same. In the midst of defeat, Jesus took the victory. He had been defeated, but he became victorious. He had been put to death, but he won the victory over death. They had put him in a tomb, but he walked out of the tomb. In the face of death, defeat, and despair, Jesus took the victory.

Because Jesus took the victory, several things come to us.

* * *

First, there is a marvelous peace greater than despair. That is what Easter means. On that first Easter when Jesus came into the room where the disciples were, he found them wanting to believe. They had been out to the tomb that morning. They saw that it was empty. Mary and the other women had told them what the angel of the Lord had said.

John, in his gospel, tells us that Jesus even appeared to Mary in the garden.

Still the disciples had not yet seen him. They wanted to believe. But they were still unsure, still hoping, still caught up in sorrow and despair. Yet they had a glimmer of hope.

Then Jesus came into the room and said to them, "Peace to you." It was the same word they had heard from him before in the calming of the storm, "Peace, be still." On their last night together he said, "My peace I leave with you." Now he assures them, "Peace to you."

That is part of the good news of Easter for us today. There is a marvelous peace greater than despair. It is "the peace of God which passes all understanding."

We need that, all of us do, for we know well the suffering of the world and people we love, the great injustices of life, the threat of disease and the certainty of death. We need the peace which is greater than despair.

This peace is never something we conjure up on our own. It is never the result of convincing ourselves that we are okay and you are okay and life is therefore okay. It is the gift of God. It comes to us through faith in a resurrected Lord.

This Easter Sunday says to us that a loving God who has created us in his own image will not leave us desolate. He will not forsake us and allow death to forever annihilate us and those we love. The peace of God in the face of death is greater than despair.

One little fellow sat in his great-grandfather's lap and said, "Grandpa, I know why you are so old. You just won't die."[3]

A young man died as a result of stress during the Vietnam war. His father had a difficult time with it. He could not let go of his son and he could find no sense of peace. He suffered for months with his sorrow. One night he had a dream in which he saw Christ embracing his son and welcoming him into the Father's house. Because of that dream he began finding peace.[4]

Maybe you saw a movie a few years ago called *Cocoon*. It is the story of some people who are going to leave the earth and live on a distant planet. It is a place far different than this world. One boy learns about this and asks his grandfather, "Why are you leaving us?" The man replies, "I'm going to a place where you never get sick, you never grow old and you never die."

> *There's a land that is fairer than day*
> *and by faith we can see it afar;*
> *for the Father waits over the way,*
> *to prepare us a dwelling place there.*[5]

Easter has a great message for us today about a marvelous peace greater than despair.

* * *

Second, there is a living proof greater than doubt. That is another thing about Easter. When those disciples heard the voice of Jesus they reacted in a way which may surprise us at first. We would expect them to be filled with faith and confidence in the face of this new reality, the appearance of their risen Lord. Instead, Luke tells us, "They were terrified and frightened, and supposed they had seen a spirit." Jesus said to them, "Why are you troubled? And why do doubts arise in your hearts? Behold my hands and my feet, that it is I myself. Handle me and see, for a spirit does not have flesh and bones as you see I have." And he showed them his hands and feet.

The living proof of his resurrection was greater than any doubt they had, greater than any fear they had. He could not be denied. He was living proof of all he had been telling them all along. He was living proof greater than doubt.

I guess all of us have some doubts sometimes. It does not mean we are being disloyal or unfaithful to God. Notice that Jesus did not scold the disciples. He simply said, "Why do you doubt? Behold my hands and my feet, that it is I myself."

We doubt only the things which are important to us, only those things we care about deeply, the ultimate concerns we care about greatly. Whenever we have doubts I have a feeling God smiles and seeks to show us more.

Frederick Buechner, a Christian writer and Presbyterian minister, wrote, "A God who leaves no room for doubt leaves no room for me."[6]

In times of doubt God reaches out to us.

A preacher was stopped for speeding. He apologized to the patrolman and said, "You wouldn't give me a ticket, would you? I'm a messenger of the Lord." The patrolman said, "I'm a messenger of the Lord, also, and I was sent here to save your life."[7]

Easter has a message for us here. It is living proof of the love, goodness, mercy, care and concern of God. It is living proof of the resurrection of Christ and our own resurrection. And this living proof is greater than our doubt.

Many years ago there was a doctor who always took his dog with him in his carriage when he went to make his calls. One day he went out to see a sick person. This man asked the doctor about his condition. The doctor told him it did not look good. They sat quietly for a while, and then the man asked, "What's it like to die, doctor?" The doctor heard his dog come up the stairs and scratch at the door. He said, "You hear that? That's my dog. He has never been in this house before. He doesn't know what's on this side of the door, but he knows his master is in here, and so he knows everything is all right. Now, death is like that. We've never been there, and we don't know what's on the other side. But, we know our Master is there. And, because of that we know everything is all right."[8]

Easter has a great message for us today about a living proof greater than doubt.

*   *   *

Third, there is a continuing presence greater than defeat. Yes, Easter means this also. The mood in the room began to change. Luke writes, "But, while they still did not believe for joy and marveled, he said to them, 'Have you any food here?' " Still they did not believe, but now it was because of their joy that such a thing could be true. They marveled. They must have thought it too good to be true. Then we read, "So, they gave Jesus a piece of fish and some honeycomb, and he took it and ate it in their presence."

He was there with them just as he had promised. Read on a little further and you will find Jesus promising he would always be with them and because of that they would be his witnesses.

The message is clear. God is greater than anything we face. This does not mean we will not face danger and will not be defeated. We will face danger and we will know defeat. That is what the cross means. Jesus was defeated. But don't forget an empty tomb overcomes a cross every time. This is the great good news of Easter and the resurrection. God is greater than anything that defeats us. God will overcome all those things and lead us beyond them.

Back in 1957 the Lutheran World Federation Assembly met in Minneapolis. One of the speakers was Bishop Ordass of Hungary. He told of how the communists had placed him in prison because of his protests against them. He said, "They placed me in solitary confinement. It was a tiny cell perhaps six feet by eight feet with no windows . . . . They hoped to break down my resistance by isolating me . . . . They thought I was alone. They were wrong. The risen Christ was present in that room, and in communion with him I was able to prevail."

Easter has a great message for us today about a continuing presence greater than defeat. It is the great message that Christ the Lord is risen today!

During one Easter season a man walked down a street and passed by a window where there was the scene of the crucifixion. A little boy was standing there looking at it. He said to the man, "Those are Roman soldiers." The man made no reply. The boy continued, "And there's Jesus." The man said nothing. The boy then said, "They killed him." The man still did not reply. He turned to walk away, but the boy grabbed his sleeve and said, "Mister, I forgot to tell you the best part. He's alive again."

That is the great message of Easter. Jesus took the victory, and because he did the victory is yours as well.

---

1. Dennis R. Fakes, *Emphasis,* CSS Publishing Co., Lima, Ohio, March-April, 1993, p. 61.

2. Charles L. Allen, *Joyful Living In The Fourth Dimension,* Fleming H. Revell Company, Old Tappan, New Jersey, 1983, p. 63.

3. A. Leonard Griffith, "The Season of Life," *Best Sermons, VOL. I,* Edited by James W. Cox, Harper & Row Publishers, San Francisco, 1988, p. 277.

4. Dallas A. Brauninger, *Emphasis,* July-August, 1992, p. 19.

5. S. F. Bennett, "Sweet By and By," *The Cokesbury Worship Hymnal,* Abingdon-Cokesbury Press, New York-Nashville, p. 199.

6. Anna Carter Florence, "Confessions Of A Doubter," *Pulpit Digest,* Harper, San Francisco, March-April, 1993, p. 5.

7. *Emphasis*, September-October, 1992, p. 59.

8. James W. Moore, *You Can Get Bitter Or Better*, Abingdon Press, Nashville, 1989, p. 27.

Our gracious Father and God of the living, on this Easter Sunday as the new light of the resurrection shines upon us may we so open our lives, our hearts and our minds to thee that this new light may shine within us.

We thank thee, Father, for the Good News of Easter, for its joy and the triumphant note of victory it places at the center of life.

We are thankful for the risen Christ and his life and death, and the way he has burst the bonds of death for us.

May our lives be so touched by the Easter Gospel that we would discover a new sense of victory over everything which would harm us.

As our Lord has been raised from the dead may we be able, by thy grace and mercy, to rise above those things which would deprive us of living.

Father, keep us from getting over this great thing that has happened. Keep us from getting used to it, and keep it alive and fresh and vital in our hearts so that our living may always be in the light of Easter and we may live victoriously.

Forgive our sins, O God, as Jesus forgave the thief on the cross who turned to him for mercy. As he found his place in paradise, so may we find ours in thee.

Father, may the world hear today the Good News of Easter, for our world needs to hear it. Break the bonds of death, destruction, and ignorance everywhere. May the news of new life and joy be heard in all the lands, for we pray in the name of our Risen Lord. Amen.

"Hail To The King"
Object: a crown

Good morning, boys and girls. I am so glad you are here in church on this Easter Sunday. This is the biggest day of the year for us. All of you look so nice in your Easter clothes today. This is the day we have been looking for all these past weeks.

Last Sunday we talked about Jesus being welcomed to Jerusalem as the new king of the Jews. But the people did not really mean that. Many people turned against him and put him to death on the cross. They laid him in a tomb on Friday. He stayed there all night, all day Saturday and all that night.

Then, on what we now call Easter Sunday, he rose up from that tomb. God brought him back to life and he stepped from that tomb out into the light of a new day.

He did not become a king after all. See this crown. It represents not just the crown of a country, but it is the crown of life, the crown of God's kingdom. Jesus is the king he was born to become.

As king he provides for us all we need. He gives us the gift of eternal life in the house of our Heavenly Father. Because of that we live forever with God and all of our family members.

All we do as a church and as Christians is based on this. This is the reason we are Christians today, because of Easter and because of what God has done in raising Jesus from the dead. Christ the Lord is risen today.

May we pray. Father, we thank you for the Good News of Easter and the gift of eternal life. In Jesus' name we pray. Amen.

Prelude

Chiming Of The Hour

Introit

The Hymn Of Praise "Christ The Lord Is Risen Today"

Affirmation Of Faith   The Apostles' Creed

Invocation

Moments Of Fellowship

Pastoral Prayer And The Lord's Prayer

The Children's Message "Hail To The King"

The Anthem "Christ Is Now Arisen"

The Prayer Of Dedication

The Offertory

The Doxology

The Hymn Of Preparation "Up From The Grave He Arose"

Scripture Lesson Luke 24:36-43

Sermon "Behold The Man Who Took The Victory"

Invitation To Christian Discipleship

Hymn Of Invitation "The Day Of Resurrection"

Benediction

The Choral Response

Postlude

1. Have someone read again the scripture lesson: Luke 24:36-43.

2. How do you understand the meaning of this passage?

3. Why were the disciples surprised by this event?

4. What did this experience do for the disciples?

5. What does the Good News of Christ's resurrection mean in your own life?

6. How can we embody the meaning of resurrection?

7. How can we best witness the power of Christ's resurrection?

Close by saying together the Apostles' Creed, with the leader pronouncing the Apostolic benediction.